Hymns for Two

Arranged by Carol Klose

ISBN 978-1-4234-0449-1

HAL•LEONARD®
CORPORATION
7777 W. BLUEMOUND RD. P.O. BOX 13819 MILWAUKEE, WI 53213

In Australia Contact:
Hal Leonard Australia Pty. Ltd.
4 Lentara Court
Cheltenham, Victoria, 3192 Australia
Email: ausadmin@halleonard.com

Visit Hal Leonard Online at
www.halleonard.com

ALL HAIL THE POWER OF JESUS' NAME

SECONDO

Words by EDWARD PERRONET
Music by OLIVER HOLDEN

Moderately, with majesty

With pedal

ALL HAIL THE POWER OF JESUS' NAME

PRIMO

Words by EDWARD PERRONET
Music by OLIVER HOLDEN

Moderately, with majesty

With pedal

SECONDO

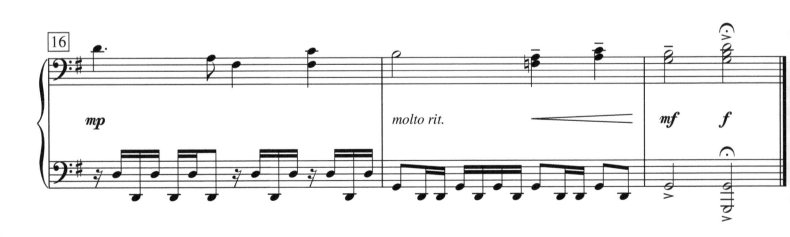

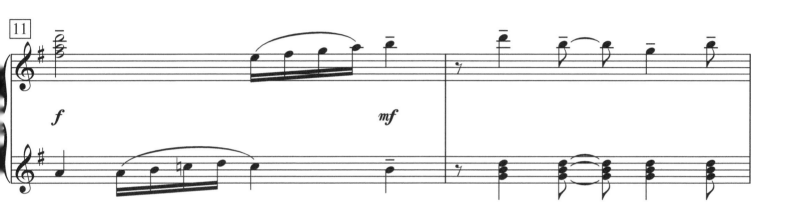

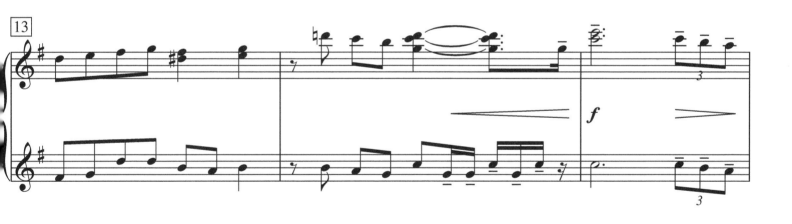

AMAZING GRACE

SECONDO

Words by JOHN NEWTON
Traditional American Melody

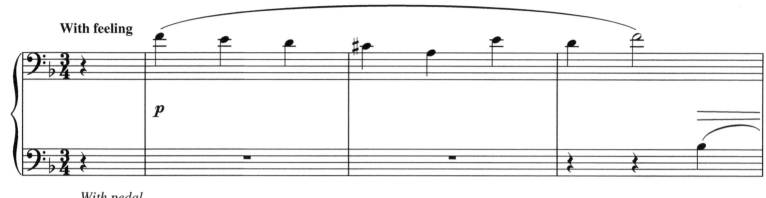

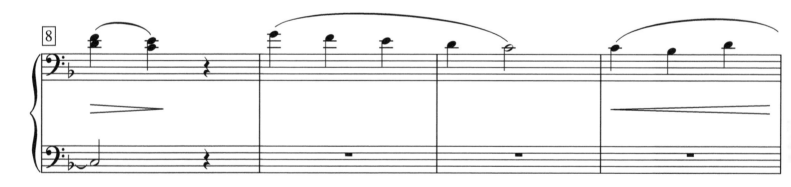

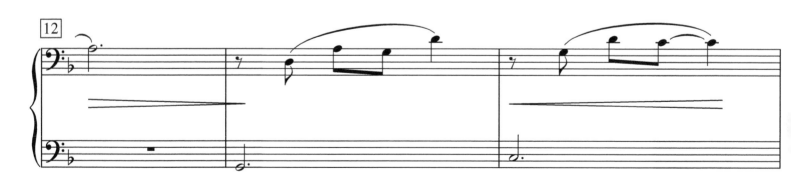

AMAZING GRACE

PRIMO

Words by JOHN NEWTON
Traditional American Melody

SECONDO

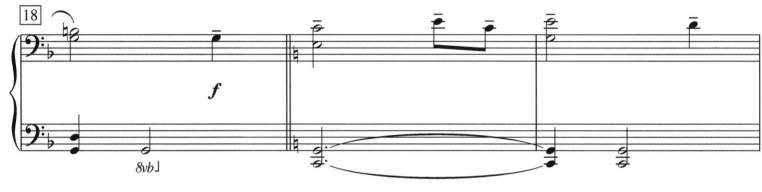

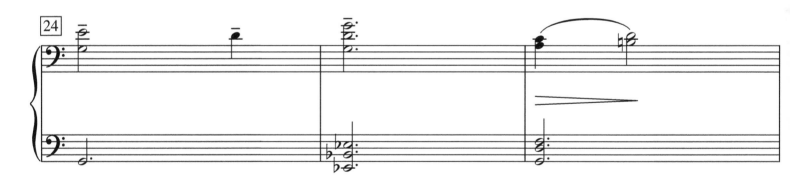

PRIMO

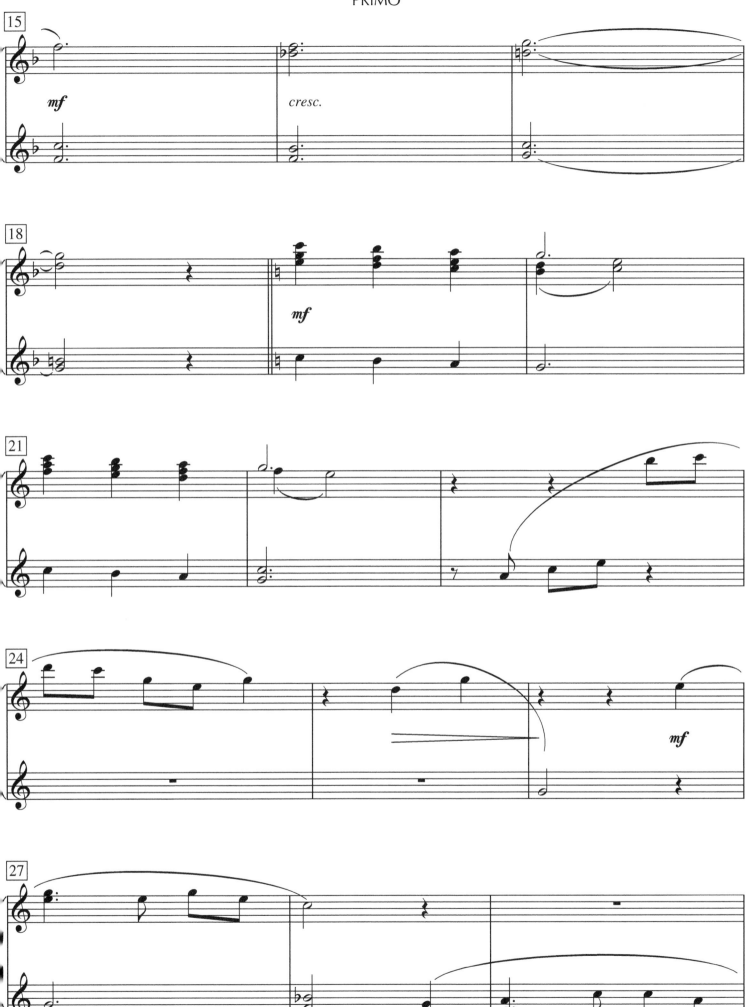

SECONDO

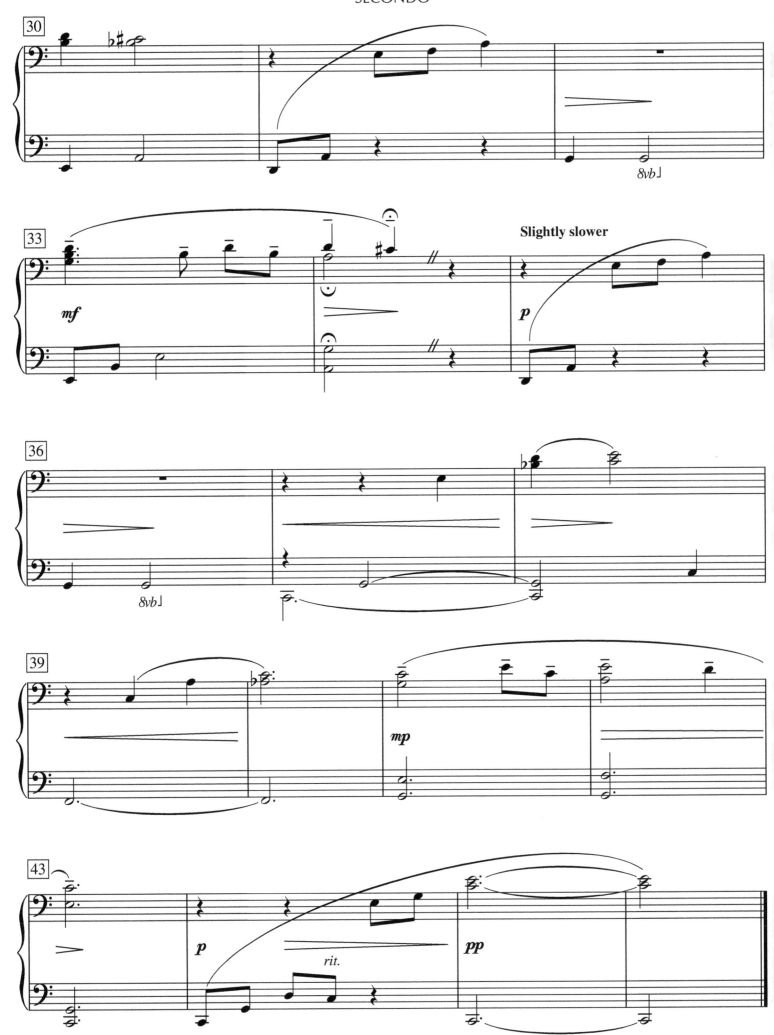

PRIMO

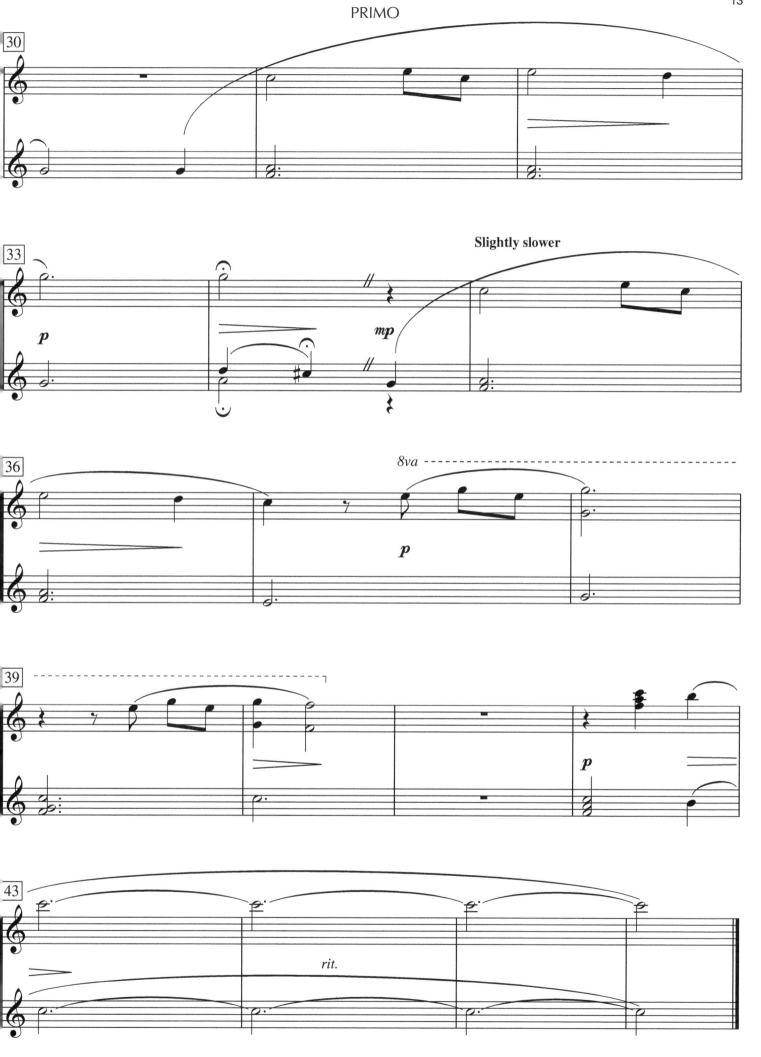

BE THOU MY VISION

SECONDO

Traditional Irish

Moderately

With pedal

BE THOU MY VISION

PRIMO

Traditional Irish

SECONDO

PRIMO

SECONDO

8vb

PRIMO

CROWN HIM WITH MANY CROWNS

SECONDO

Words by MATTHEW BRIDGES and GODFREY THRING
Music by GEORGE JOB ELVEY

CROWN HIM WITH MANY CROWNS

PRIMO

Words by MATTHEW BRIDGES and GODFREY THRING
Music by GEORGE JOB ELVEY

With majesty

With pedal

SECONDO

FAIREST LORD JESUS

SECONDO

Words from *Munster Gesangbuch*
Music from *Schlesische Volkslieder*

Slowly, with dignity

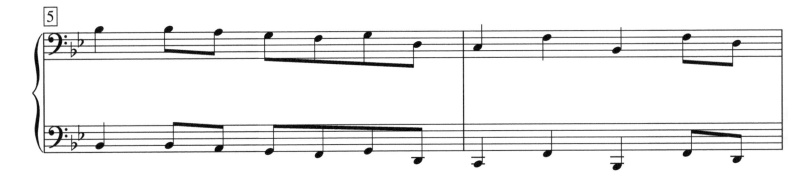

FAIREST LORD JESUS

PRIMO

Words from *Munster Gesangbuch*
Music from *Schlesische Volkslieder*

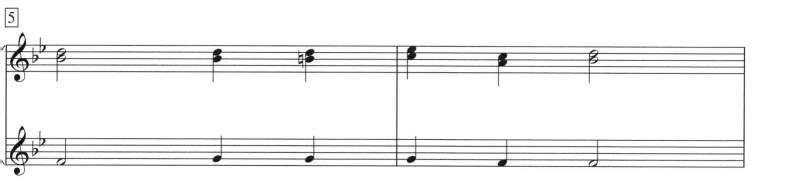

SECONDO

HOLY, HOLY, HOLY

SECONDO

Words by REGINALD HEBER
Music by JOHN B. DYKES

HOLY, HOLY, HOLY

PRIMO

Words by REGINALD HEBER
Music by JOHN B. DYKES

With great fanfare

SECONDO

I NEED THEE EVERY HOUR

SECONDO

Words by ANNIE S. HAWKS
Music by ROBERT LOWRY

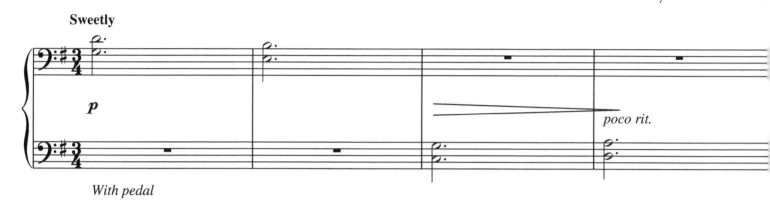

I NEED THEE EVERY HOUR

PRIMO

Words by ANNIE S. HAWKS
Music by ROBERT LOWRY

SECONDO

PRIMO

I SING THE MIGHTY POWER OF GOD

SECONDO

Words by ISAAC WATTS
Music from *Gesangbuch der Herzog*

Moderately

Opt. pedal

I SING THE MIGHTY POWER OF GOD

PRIMO

Words by ISAAC WATTS
Music from *Gesangbuch der Herzogl*

PRIMO

O WORSHIP THE KING

SECONDO

Words by ROBERT GRANT
Music attributed to JOHANN MICHAEL HAYDN

Moderately, with expression

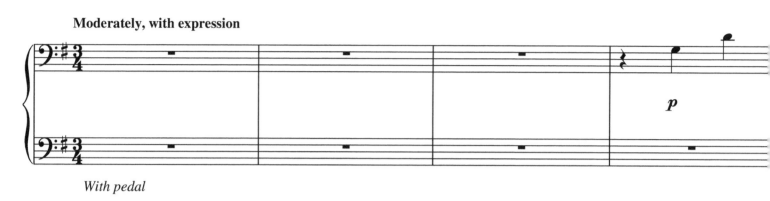

With pedal

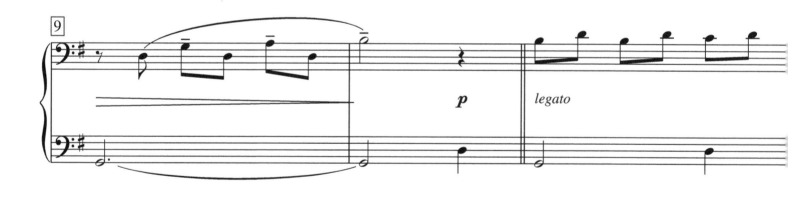

O WORSHIP THE KING

PRIMO

Words by ROBERT GRANT
Music attributed to JOHANN MICHAEL HAYDN

SECONDO

PRIMO

SPIRIT OF GOD, DESCEND UPON MY HEART

SECONDO

Words by GEORGE CROLY
Music by FREDERICK COOK ATKINSON

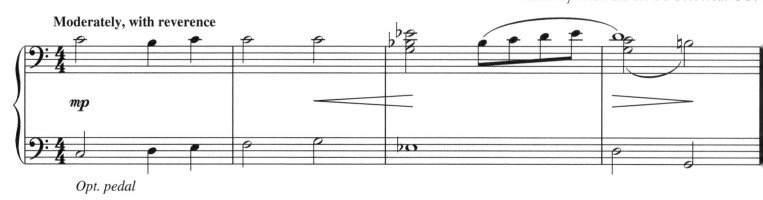

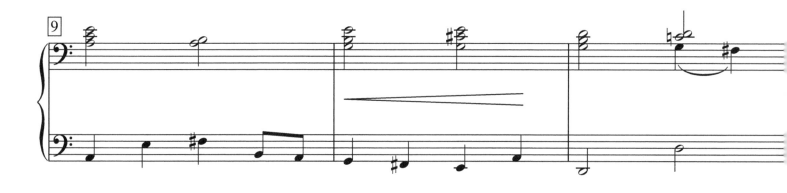

SPIRIT OF GOD, DESCEND UPON MY HEART

PRIMO

Words by GEORGE CROLY
Music by FREDERICK COOK ATKINSON

SECONDO

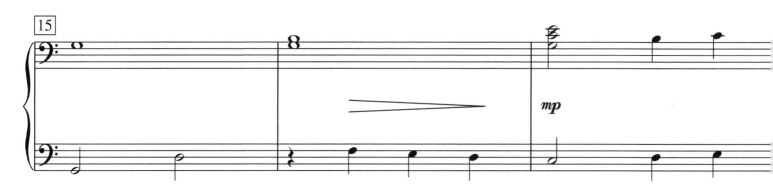

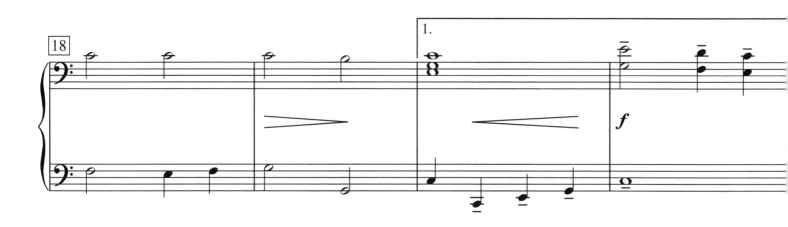

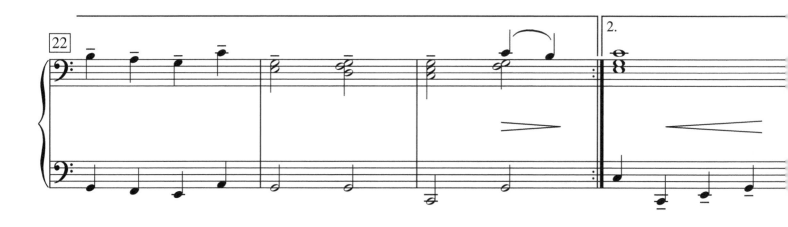

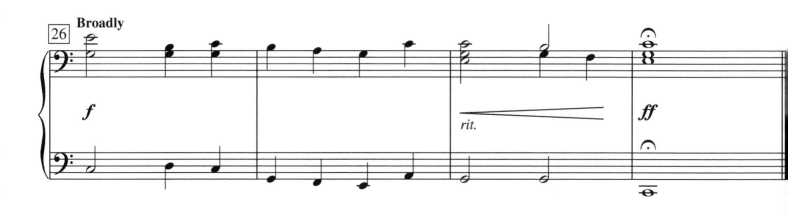

PRIMO

TO GOD BE THE GLORY

SECONDO

Words by FANNY J. CROSBY
Music by WILLIAM H. DOANE

TO GOD BE THE GLORY

PRIMO

Words by FANNY J. CROSBY
Music by WILLIAM H. DOANE

SECONDO

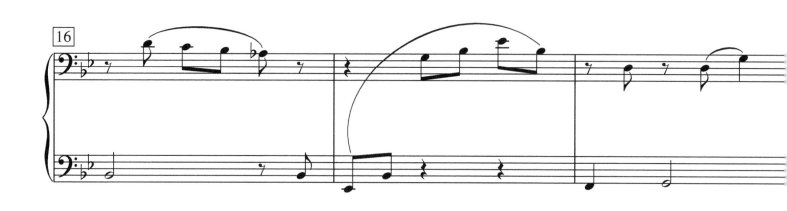

PRIMO

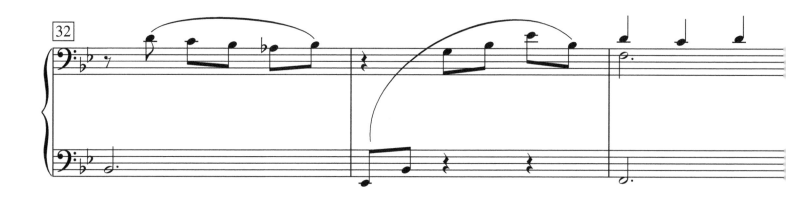

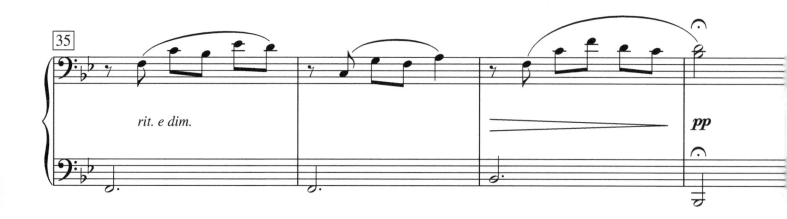

PRIMO

WHAT A FRIEND WE HAVE IN JESUS

SECONDO

Words by JOSEPH M. SCRIVE
Music by CHARLES C. CONVERS

Moderately

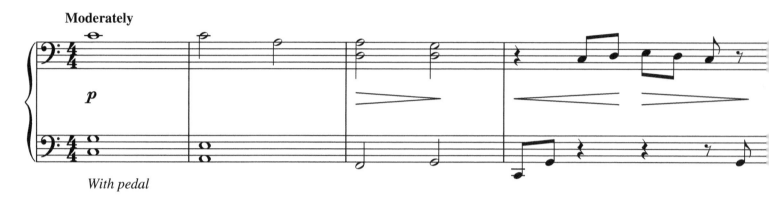

With pedal

WHAT A FRIEND WE HAVE IN JESUS

PRIMO

Words by JOSEPH M. SCRIVEN
Music by CHARLES C. CONVERSE

SECONDO

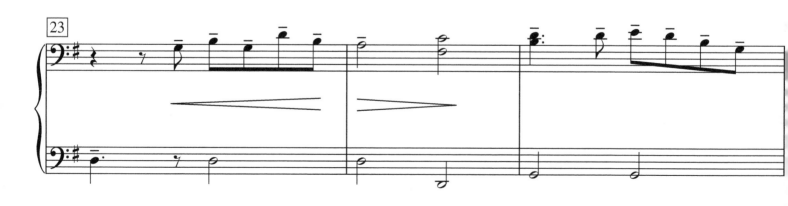

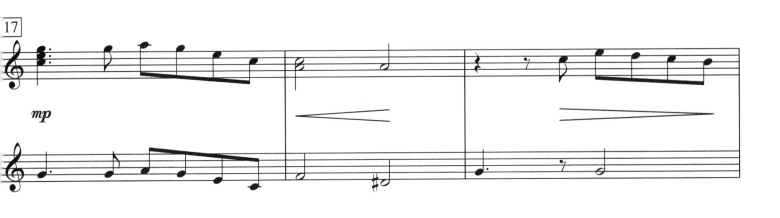

62

SECONDO

The Best
Sacred Collections

for Piano

Blended Worship Piano Collection

Songs include: Amazing Grace (My Chains Are Gone) • Be Thou My Vision • I Will Rise • Joyful, Joyful, We Adore Thee • Lamb of God • Majesty • Open the Eyes of My Heart • Praise to the Lord, the Almighty • Shout to the Lord • 10,000 Reasons (Bless the Lord) • Worthy Is the Lamb • Your Name • and more.
00293528 Piano Solo $17.99

Hymn Anthology

A beautiful collection of 60 hymns arranged for piano solo, including: Abide with Me • Be Thou My Vision • Come, Thou Fount of Every Blessing • Doxology • For the Beauty of the Earth • God of Grace and God of Glory • Holy, Holy, Holy • It Is Well with My Soul • Joyful, Joyful, We Adore Thee • Let Us Break Bread Together • A Mighty Fortress Is Our God • O God, Our Help in Ages Past • Savior, like a Shepherd Lead Us • To God Be the Glory • What a Friend We Have in Jesus • and more.
00251244 Piano Solo $16.99

The Hymn Collection

arranged by Phillip Keveren

17 beloved hymns expertly and beautifully arranged for solo piano by Phillip Keveren. Includes: All Hail the Power of Jesus' Name • I Love to Tell the Story • I Surrender All • I've Got Peace Like a River • Were You There? • and more.
00311071 Piano Solo $14.99

Hymn Duets

arranged by Phillip Keveren

Includes lovely duet arrangements of: All Creatures of Our God and King • I Surrender All • It Is Well with My Soul • O Sacred Head, Now Wounded • Praise to the Lord, The Almighty • Rejoice, The Lord Is King • and more.
00311544 Piano Duet $14.99

Hymn Medleys

arranged by Phillip Keveren

Great medleys resonate with the human spirit, as do the truths in these moving hymns. Here Phillip Keveren combines 24 timeless favorites into eight lovely medleys for solo piano.
00311349 Piano Solo $14.99

P/V/G = Piano/Vocal/Guitar arrangements.

Prices, contents and availability subject to change without notice.

Hymns for Two

arranged by Carol Klose

12 piano duet arrangements of favorite hymns: Amazing Grace • Be Thou My Vision • Crown Him with Many Crowns • Fairest Lord Jesus • Holy, Holy, Holy • I Need Thee Every Hour • O Worship the King • What a Friend We Have in Jesus • and more.
00290544 Piano Duet $12.99

It Is Well

10 BELOVED HYMNS FOR MEMORIAL SERVICES
arr. John Purifoy

10 peaceful, soul-stirring hymn settings appropriate for memorial services and general worship use. Titles include: Abide with Me • Amazing Grace • Be Still My Soul • For All the Saints • His Eye Is on the Sparrow • In the Garden • It Is Well with My Soul • Like a River Glorious • Rock of Ages • What a Friend We Have in Jesus.
00118920 Piano Solo $12.99

Ragtime Gospel Classics

arr. Steven K. Tedesco

A dozen old-time gospel favorites: Because He Lives • Goodbye World Goodbye • He Touched Me • I Saw the Light • I'll Fly Away • Keep on the Firing Line • Mansion over the Hilltop • No One Ever Cared for Me like Jesus • There Will Be Peace in the Valley for Me • Victory in Jesus • What a Day That Will Be • Where Could I Go.
00142449 Piano Solo $11.99

Ragtime Gospel Hymns

arranged by Steven Tedesco

15 traditional gospel hymns, including: At Calvary • Footsteps of Jesus • Just a Closer Walk with Thee • Leaning on the Everlasting Arms • What a Friend We Have in Jesus • When We All Get to Heaven • and more.
00311763 Piano Solo $10.99

Sacred Classics for Solo Piano

arr. John Purifoy

10 timeless songs of faith, masterfully arranged by John Purifoy. Because He Lives • Easter Song • Glorify Thy Name • Here Am I, Send Me • I'd Rather Have Jesus • Majesty • On Eagle's Wings • There's Something About That Name • We Shall Behold Him • Worthy Is the Lamb.
00141703 Piano Solo $14.99

Raise Your Hands

PIANO SOLOS FOR BLENDED WORSHIP
arr. Heather Sorenson

10 uplifting and worshipful solos crafted by Heather Sorenson. Come Thou Fount, Come Thou King • God of Heaven • Holy Is the Lord (with "Holy, Holy, Holy") • Holy Spirit I Will Rise • In Christ Alone • Raise Your Hands • Revelation Song • 10,000 Reasons (Bless the Lord) • Your Name (with "All Hail the Power of Jesus' Name").
00231579 Piano Solo $14.99

Seasonal Sunday Solos for Piano

24 blended selections grouped by occasion. Includes Breath of Heaven (Mary's Song) • Come, Ye Thankful People, Come • Do You Hear What I Hear • God of Our Fathers • In the Name of the Lord • Mary, Did You Know? • Mighty to Save • Spirit of the Living God • The Wonderful Cross • and more.
00311971 Piano Solo $16.99

Sunday Solos for Piano

30 blended selections, perfect for the church pianist. Songs include: All Hail the Power of Jesus' Name • Be Thou My Vision • Great Is the Lord • Here I Am to Worship • Majesty • Open the Eyes of My Heart • and many more.
00311272 Piano Solo $17.99

More Sunday Solos for Piano

A follow-up to *Sunday Solos for Piano*, this collection features 30 more blended selections perfect for the church pianist. Includes: Agnus Dei • Come, Thou Fount of Every Blessing • The Heart of Worship • How Great Thou Art • Immortal, Invisible • O Worship the King • Shout to the Lord • Thy Word • We Fall Down • and more.
00311864 Piano Solo $16.99

Even More Sunday Solos for Piano

30 blended selections, including: Ancient Words • Brethren, We Have Met to Worship • How Great Is Our God • Lead On, O King Eternal • Offering • Savior, Like a Shepherd Lead Us • We Bow Down • Worthy of Worship • and more.
00312098 Piano Solo $16.99

0122
001